Cram101 Textbook Outlines to accompany:

Women, Men, and Society

Renzetti & Curran, 5th Edition

An Academic Internet Publishers (AIPI) publication (c) 2007.

You have a discounted membership at www.Cram101.com with this book.

Get all of the practice tests for the chapters of this textbook, and access in-depth reference material for writing essays and papers. Here is an example from a Cram101 Biology text:

When you need problem solving help with math, stats, and other disciplines, www.Cram101.com will walk through the formulas and solutions step by step.

With Cram101.com online, you also have access to extensive reference material.

You will nail those essays and papers. Here is an example from a Cram101 Biology text:

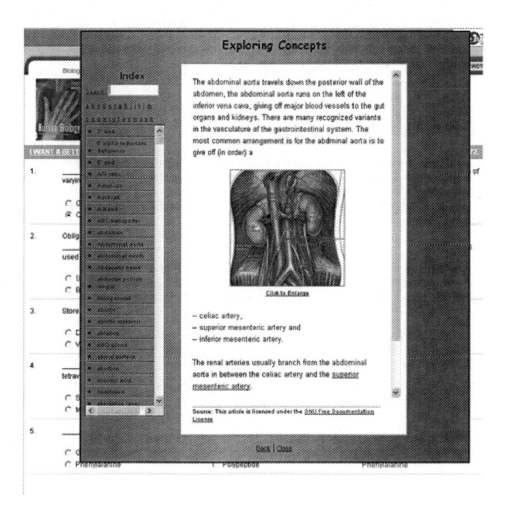

Learning System

Cram101 Textbook Outlines is a learning system. The notes in this book are the highlights of your textbook, you will never have to highlight a book again.

How to use this book. Take this book to class, it is your notebook for the lecture. The notes and highlights on the left hand side of the pages follow the outline and order of the textbook. All you have to do is follow along while your intructor presents the lecture. Circle the items emphasized in class and add other important information on the right side. With Cram101 Textbook Outlines you'll spend less time writing and more time listening. Learning becomes more efficient.

Cram101.com Online

Increase your studying efficiency by using Cram101.com's practice tests and online reference material. It is the perfect complement to Cram101 Textbook Outlines. Use self-teaching matching tests or simulate in-class testing with comprehensive multiple choice tests, or simply use Cram's true and false tests for quick review. Cram101.com even allows you to enter your in-class notes for an integrated studying format combining the textbook notes with your class notes.

Visit **www.Cram101.com**, click Sign Up at the top of the screen, and enter **DK73DW255** in the promo code box on the registration screen. Access to www.Cram101.com is normally $9.95, but because you have purchased this book, your access fee is only $4.95. Sign up and stop highlighting textbooks forever.

Women, Men, and Society
Renzetti & Curran, 5th

CONTENTS

Gender	Gender refers to socially defined behavior regarded as appropriate for the members of each sex.
Masculinity	Masculinity refers to the characteristic forms of behavior expected of men in any given culture.
Femininity	Femininity comprises the physical and mental attributes associated with the female sex and is partly culturally determined.
Stereotype	A stereotype refers to widely shared beliefs about the characteristic traits, attitudes, and behaviors of members of various social groups, including the assumption that the members of such groups are usually all alike.
Society	A society is a grouping of individuals, which is characterized by common interest and may have distinctive culture and institutions.
Social interaction	Social interaction is a dynamic, changing sequence of social actions between individuals (or groups) who modify their actions and reactions due to the actions by their interaction partner(s). In other words they are events in which people attach meaning to a situation, interpret what others are meaning, and respond accordingly.
Social stratification	The systematic, uneven distribution of valued products of social life such as wealth, power, and prestige among the occupants of different social statuses, is referred to as a social stratification.
Social institution	Social institution is a group of social positions, connected by social relations, performing a social role. It can be also defined in a narrow sense as any institution in a society that works to socialize the groups or people in it.
Life chances	Life chances are the opportunities each individual has to improve their quality of life. The concept was introduced by German sociologist Max Weber. It is a probabilistic concept, describing how likely it is, given certain factors, that an individual's life will turn out a certain way.
Patriarchy	Patriarchy is the anthropological term used to define the sociological condition where male members of a society tend to predominate in positions of power; with the more powerful the position, the more likely it is that a male will hold that position.
Paradigm	In social science, paradigm is used to describe the set of experiences, beliefs and values that affect the way an individual perceives reality and responds to that perception.
Functionalism	In the social sciences, specifically sociology and sociocultural anthropology, functionalism, also called functional analysis, is a sociological perspective that originally attempted to explain social institutions as collective means to fill individual biological needs. Later, it came to focus on the ways in which social institutions fill social needs, especially social stability.
Societal consensus	A situation whereby the majority of members share a common set of values, beliefs, and behavioral expectations is a societal consensus.
Consensus	Agreement on basic social values by the members of a group or society is referred to as a consensus.
Social change	Social change refers to alteration in social structures or culture over time.
Gender role	A gender role is a set of behavioral norms associated with males and with females, respectively, in a given social group or system.
Social role	A social role is a set of connected behaviors, rights and obligations as conceptualized by actors in a social situation. It is mostly defined as an expected behavior in a given individual social status and social position.
Norm	In sociology, a norm, or social norm, is a rule that is socially enforced. Social sanctioning is what distinguishes norms from other cultural products such as meaning and values.
Discrimination	Discrimination refers to the denial of equal access to social resources to people on the basis of their group membership.

Social learning	The process through which we acquire new information, forms of behavior, or attitudes exclusively or primarily in a social group, is referred to as a social learning.
Status quo	Status quo is a Latin term meaning the present, current, existing state of affairs. To maintain the status quo is to keep things the way they presently are.
Collective action	Collective action is the pursuit of a goal or set of goals by more than one person.
Civil rights	Civil rights are the protections and privileges of personal liberty given to all citizens by law. Civil rights are rights that are bestowed by nations on those within their territorial boundaries.
Feminism	Feminism is a diverse collection of social theories, political movements and moral philosophies, largely motivated by or concerned with the experiences of women.
Acquisition	The initial learning of the stimulus response link, which involves a neutral stimulus being associated with a UCS and becoming a conditioned stimulus, is referred to as an acquisition.
Range	A measure of variability defined as the high score in a distribution minus the low score is referred to as a range.
Bias	A bias is a prejudice in a general or specific sense, usually in the sense for having a preference to one particular point of view or ideological perspective.
Sexism	Sexism is commonly considered to be discrimination and/or hatred against people based on their sex rather than their individual merits, but can also refer to any and all systemic differentiations based on the sex of the individuals.
Prejudice	Prejudice is, as the name implies, the process of "pre-judging" something. It implies coming to a judgment on a subject before learning where the preponderance of evidence actually lies, or forming a judgment without direct experience.
Attitude	Attitude refers to an enduring mental representation of a person, place, or thing that evokes an emotional response and related behavior.
Urban sociology	Urban sociology is the sociological study of the various statistics among the population in cities. Chiefly the study of urban areas where industrial, commercial and residental zones converge.
Neighborhood	A neighborhood is a geographically localized community located within a larger city, town or suburb. Traditionally, a neighborhood is small enough that the neighbors are all able to know each other.
Community	Community refers to a group of people who share a common sense of identity and interact with one another on a sustained basis.
Social structure	The term social structure, used in a general sense, refers to entities or groups in definite relation to each other, to relatively enduring patterns of behavior and relationship within social systems, or to social institutions and norms becoming embedded into social systems in such a way that they shape the behavior of actors within those social systems.
Research methods	The diverse strategies used to gather empirical material in a systematic way are research methods.
Social construction	A social construction is an institutionalized entity or artifact in a social system 'invented' or 'constructed' by participants in a particular culture or society that exists solely because people agree to behave as if it exists, or agree to follow certain conventional rules.
Organization	In sociology organization is understood as planned, coordinated and purposeful action of human beings to construct or compile a common tangible or intangible product or service.
Racism	Racism is a belief in the moral or biological superiority of one race or ethnic group over another or others.
Ageism	Ageism refers to prejudice against a person on the grounds of age in the belief that the age category

is inferior to other age categories and that unequal treatment is therefore justified.

Group consciousness	Group consciousness refers to an awareness that an individual's problems are shared by others who are similarly situated in regard to race/ethnicity, gender, class, or age.
Consciousness	The awareness of the senzations, thoughts, and feelings being experienced at a given moment is referred to as consciousness.
Social inequality	The fact that critical aspects of life such as economic benefits, life chances, social privileges, and political power are unequally distributed in society, is referred to as a social inequality.
Feminist movement	The collective activities of individuals, groups, and organizations whose goal is the fair and equal treatment of women and men around the world is a feminist movement. They campaign on issues such as reproductive rights (including abortion), domestic violence, maternity leave, equal pay, sexual harassment, and sexual violence.
Feminist theory	Theory or perspective that focuses on male dominance in families and society and examines how gender differences are related to power differentials between men and women is a feminist theory.
Social movement	A social movement refers to large informal groupings of individuals and/or organizations focused on specific political or social issues, in other words, on carrying out, resisting or undoing a social change.
Individualism	Putting personal goals ahead of group goals and defining one's identity in terms of personal attributes rather than group memberships is individualism.
Ideology	Ideology refers to shared ideas or beliefs which serve to justify and support the interests of a particular group or organizations.
Hypocrisy	Publicly advocating some attitude or behavior and then acting in a way that is inconsistent with this espoused attitude or behavior, is referred to as hypocrisy.
Marxism	Marxism refers to the philosophy and social theory based on Karl Marx's work on one hand, and to the political practice based on Marxist theory on the other hand (namely, parts of the First International during Marx's time, communist parties and later states).
Government	A government is a body that has the authority to make and the power to enforce laws within a civil, corporate, religious, academic, or other organization or group.
Labeling	Labeling is defining or describing a person in terms of his or her behavior. The term is often used in sociology to describe human interaction, control and identification of deviant behavior.
Social problem	A social condition that is perceived as having harmful effects is a social problem. Opinions about whether a condition is a social problem vary among groups and depend upon how and by whom the condition is defined and perceived in society.
Public sphere	Public sphere refers to the means by which people communicate in modern societies, the most prominent component of which is mass media-movies, television, radio, videos, records, magazines, and newspapers.
Abortion	An abortion is the removal or expulsion of an embryo or fetus from the uterus, resulting in, or caused by, its death. This can occur spontaneously as a miscarriage, or be artificially induced through chemical, surgical or other means. Commonly, " abortion " refers to an induced procedure at any point in the pregnancy; medically, it is defined as a miscarriage or induced termination before twenty weeks gestation, which is considered nonviable.
Contradiction	Marx's term to refer to mutually antagonistic tendencies within institutions or the broader society such as those between profit and competition within capitalism is referred to as a contradiction.
Rape	Rape is the act of forcing penetrative sexual acts, against another's will through violence, force, threat of injury, or other duress, or where the victim is unable to decline, due to the effects of drugs or alcohol.

7

Liberal feminism	A branch of feminism that argues that gender equality can he achieved without challenging men as a group or changing basic economic and political arrangements such as capitalism is a liberal feminism.
Dominance	In animal colonies, a condition established by one animal over another by prevailing in an aggressive encounter between the two, is referred to as dominance.
Radical feminism	A branch of feminism that argues that patriarchy centers on a fundamental difference in interests between men and women, and that equality for women cannot be achieved unless men collectively give up the power, wealth, and privilege that patriarchy grants them, is referred to as radical feminism.
Social class	A category of people who occupy a similar position in relation to the means through which goods and services are produced in a society is a social class.
Sexual orientation	Sexual orientation describes the direction of an individual's sexuality, often in relation to their own sex or gender. Common terms for describing sexual orientation include bisexual (bi), heterosexual (straight) and homosexual (lesbian/gay).
Censorship	The practice of suppressing material that is considered morally, politically, or otherwise objectionable is referred to as censorship.
Stigmatized	People who have been negatively labeled because of their participation, or alleged participation, in deviant or outlawed behaviors are referred to as stigmatized.
Sexual harassment	Sexual harassment refers to the making of persistent unwanted sexual advances by one individual towards another.
Murder	Murder is the unlawful, premeditated killing of a human being by another. The penalty for murder is usually either life imprisonment, or in jurisdictions with capital punishment, the death penalty.
Affirmative action	Government programs intended to assure minorities and women equal hiring or admission opportunities is referred to as affirmative action.
Middle class	A social class broadly defined occupationally as those working in white-collar and lower managerial occupations and is sometimes defined by reference to income levels or subjective identification of the participants in the study are referred to as middle class.
Homophobia	Homophobia is the fear of, aversion to, or discrimination against homosexuality or homosexuals. It can also mean hatred, hostility, or disapproval of homosexual people, sexual behavior, or cultures, and is generally used to assert bigotry.

8

Go to **Cram101.com** for the Practice Tests for this Chapter.

Attitude	Attitude refers to an enduring mental representation of a person, place, or thing that evokes an emotional response and related behavior.
Gender	Gender refers to socially defined behavior regarded as appropriate for the members of each
Organization	In sociology organization is understood as planned, coordinated and purposeful action of human beings to construct or compile a common tangible or intangible product or service.
Androgen	Androgen is the generic term for any natural or synthetic compound, usually a steroid hormone, that stimulates or controls the development and maintenance of masculine characteristics in vertebrates by binding to androgen receptors. This includes the activity of the accessory male sex organs and development of male secondary sex characteristics.
Femininity	Femininity comprises the physical and mental attributes associated with the female sex and is partly culturally determined.
Socialization	Socialization refers to the lifelong processes through which humans develop an awareness of social norms and values, and achieve a distinct sense of self.
Society	A society is a grouping of individuals, which is characterized by common interest and may have distinctive culture and institutions.
Frequency	In statistics the frequency of an event i is the number n_i of times the event occurred in the experiment or the study.
Murder	Murder is the unlawful, premeditated killing of a human being by another. The penalty for murder is usually either life imprisonment, or in jurisdictions with capital punishment, the death penalty.
Community	Community refers to a group of people who share a common sense of identity and interact with one another on a sustained basis.
Bisexual	Bisexual is the sexual orientation which refers to the aesthetic, romantic, or sexual desire for individuals of either gender or of either sex.
Social class	A category of people who occupy a similar position in relation to the means through which goods and services are produced in a society is a social class.
Gender identity	Gender identity describes the gender with which a person identifies, but can also be used to refer to the gender that other people attribute to the individual on the basis of what they know from gender role indications
Bias	A bias is a prejudice in a general or specific sense, usually in the sense for having a preference to one particular point of view or ideological perspective.
Masculinity	Masculinity refers to the characteristic forms of behavior expected of men in any given culture.
Technology	The application of logic, reason and knowledge to the problems of exploiting raw materials from the environment, is referred to as a technology.
Norm	In sociology, a norm, or social norm, is a rule that is socially enforced. Social sanctioning is what distinguishes norms from other cultural products such as meaning and values.
Stigmatized	People who have been negatively labeled because of their participation, or alleged participation, in deviant or outlawed behaviors are referred to as stigmatized.
Sexual orientation	Sexual orientation describes the direction of an individual's sexuality, often in relation to their own sex or gender. Common terms for describing sexual orientation include bisexual (bi), heterosexual (straight) and homosexual (lesbian/gay).
Feedback loop	Sociocultural materialism term referring to the dynamic relationships between the different

	components of a sociocultural system is a feedback loop. A feedback loop is a system where outputs are fed back into the system as inputs, increasing or decreasing effects.
Dominance	In animal colonies, a condition established by one animal over another by prevailing in an aggressive encounter between the two, is referred to as dominance.
Dopamine	Dopamine refers to a neurotransmitter that functions in the parts of the brain that control emotions and bodily movement.
Reinforcement	A stimulus that follows a response and increases the frequency of the response is a reinforcement.
Stereotype	A stereotype refers to widely shared beliefs about the characteristic traits, attitudes, and behaviors of members of various social groups, including the assumption that the members of such groups are usually all alike.
Manslaughter	Manslaughter refers to the killing of another person through gross negligence or without specific intent.
Probation	Nonpunitive, legal disposition of juveniles emphasizing community treatment in which the juvenile is closely supervized by an officer of the court and must adhere to a strict set of rules to avoid incarceration is probation.
Crime	Crime refers to any action that violates criminal laws established by political authority. A crime in a nontechnical sense is an act that violates a very important political or moral command.
Retrospective studies	Retrospective studies refers to a procedure by which a researcher examines data available prior to the beginning of the study to answer the research question.
Consensus	Agreement on basic social values by the members of a group or society is referred to as a consensus.
Biological Determinism	Biological determinism is the hypothesis that biological factors such as an organism's individual genes (as opposed to social or environmental factors) completely determine how a system behaves or changes over time.
Determinism	Determinism is the philosophical proposition that every event, including human cognition and action, is causally determined by an unbroken chain of prior occurrences. No wholly random, spontaneous, mysterious, or miraculous events occur, according to this philosophy.
Motive	Motive refers to a hypothetical state within an organism that propels the organism toward a goal. In criminal law a motive is the cause that moves people and induce a certain action.

12

Go to **Cram101.com** for the Practice Tests for this Chapter.

Popular culture	The component of culture that consists of activities, products, and services that are assumed to appeal primarily to members of the middle and working classes, is referred to as a popular culture.
Reconstruction	Reconstruction refers to a memory that is not an exact replica of an event but has been pieced together from a few highlights, using information that may or may not be accurate.
Nuclear family	The term nuclear family was developed in the western world to distinguish the family group consisting of parents and their children, usually a father, mother, and children, from what is known as an extended family.
Anthropology	A social science, closely linked to sociology, which concentrates on the study of traditional cultures--particularly hunting and gathering, horticultural societies, and the evolution of the human species is referred to as anthropology.
Society	A society is a grouping of individuals, which is characterized by common interest and may have distinctive culture and institutions.
Bias	A bias is a prejudice in a general or specific sense, usually in the sense for having a preference to one particular point of view or ideological perspective.
Ethnocentrism	The tendency to judge other cultures by the standards of one's own culture is ethnocentrism.
Gender	Gender refers to socially defined behavior regarded as appropriate for the members of each
Technology	The application of logic, reason and knowledge to the problems of exploiting raw materials from the environment, is referred to as a technology.
Gender role	A gender role is a set of behavioral norms associated with males and with females, respectively, in a given social group or system.
Adaptation	Adaptation refers to the ability of a sociocultural system to change with the demands of a changing physical or social environment.
Attribution	Attribution is also a psychological concept. When people watch the world, they do not see it as a completely random stream of happenings, but tend to attribute meanings to things. So, for example when you see someone fall over, you can attribute this to a stable trait, or to a feature of the situation, or to random chance.
Stereotype	A stereotype refers to widely shared beliefs about the characteristic traits, attitudes, and behaviors of members of various social groups, including the assumption that the members of such groups are usually all alike.
Government	A government is a body that has the authority to make and the power to enforce laws within a civil, corporate, religious, academic, or other organization or group.
Dominance	In animal colonies, a condition established by one animal over another by prevailing in an aggressive encounter between the two, is referred to as dominance.
Organization	In sociology organization is understood as planned, coordinated and purposeful action of human beings to construct or compile a common tangible or intangible product or service.
Acquisition	The initial learning of the stimulus response link, which involves a neutral stimulus being associated with a UCS and becoming a conditioned stimulus, is referred to as an acquisition.
Cultural universal	A cultural universal is an element, pattern, trait or institution that is common to all human cultures on the planet.
Division of labor	Division of labor is the specialisation of cooperative labor in specific, circumscribed tasks and roles, intended to increase efficiency of output.
Community	Community refers to a group of people who share a common sense of identity and interact with

one another on a sustained basis.

Prestige	Prestige refers to social respect accorded to an individual or group because of the status of their position.
Interdependence	Interdependence is a dynamic of being mutually responsible to and sharing a common set of principles with others. This concept differs dinstinctly from "dependence" in that an interdependent relationship implies that all participants are emotionally, economically, and/or morally "independent."
Horticultural society	Horticultural society refers to a society in which subsistence needs are met primarily through cultivation of small gardens without the use of advanced technology. This type of society is preindustrial and must be located in an area where conditions are suitable for growing crops reliably.
Ritual	A ritual is a set of actions, performed mainly for their symbolic value, which is prescribed by a religion or by the traditions of a community.
Range	A measure of variability defined as the high score in a distribution minus the low score is referred to as a range.
Reciprocity	In social psychology, reciprocity refers to in-kind positive or negative responses of individuals towards the actions of others. Thus positively interpreted actions elicit positive responses and vice versa.
Variable	A characteristic that varies in value or magnitude along which an object, individual or group may be categorized, such as income or age, is referred to as a variable.
Shamanism	Shamanism refers to a range of traditional beliefs and practices similar to Animism that claim the ability to diagnose and cure human suffering and, in some societies, the ability to cause suffering. This is believed to be accomplished by traversing the axis mundi and forming a special relationship with, or gaining control over, spirits.
Transsexual	A person who has the genitals of one sex but the gender identity of the other, is referred to as a transsexual.
Motive	Motive refers to a hypothetical state within an organism that propels the organism toward a goal. In criminal law a motive is the cause that moves people and induce a certain action.
Sexual orientation	Sexual orientation describes the direction of an individual's sexuality, often in relation to their own sex or gender. Common terms for describing sexual orientation include bisexual (bi), heterosexual (straight) and homosexual (lesbian/gay).
Attitude	Attitude refers to an enduring mental representation of a person, place, or thing that evokes an emotional response and related behavior.
Femininity	Femininity comprises the physical and mental attributes associated with the female sex and is partly culturally determined.
Authority	Authority refers to power that is attached to a position that others perceive as legitimate.
Masculinity	Masculinity refers to the characteristic forms of behavior expected of men in any given culture.

Stereotype	A stereotype refers to widely shared beliefs about the characteristic traits, attitudes, and behaviors of members of various social groups, including the assumption that the members of such groups are usually all alike.
Gender	Gender refers to socially defined behavior regarded as appropriate for the members of each
Socialization	Socialization refers to the lifelong processes through which humans develop an awareness of social norms and values, and achieve a distinct sense of self.
Norm	In sociology, a norm, or social norm, is a rule that is socially enforced. Social sanctioning is what distinguishes norms from other cultural products such as meaning and values.
Gender socialization	Gender socialization refers to the aspect of socialization that contains specific messages and practices concerning the nature of being female or male in a specific group or society.
Peer group	A friendship group with common interests and position composed of individuals of similar age is referred to as a peer group.
Social learning	The process through which we acquire new information, forms of behavior, or attitudes exclusively or primarily in a social group, is referred to as a social learning.
Developmental theories	Those that assert that personal characteristics guide human development and influence behavioral choices but that these choices may change over the life course are called developmental theories.
Gender identity	Gender identity describes the gender with which a person identifies, but can also be used to refer to the gender that other people attribute to the individual on the basis of what they know from gender role indications
Castration	Castration is any action, surgical, chemical, or otherwise, by which a biological male loses use of the testes. A temporary chemical castration has been studied and developed as a preventive measure and punishment for several repeated sex crimes such as rape or other sexually related violence.
Community	Community refers to a group of people who share a common sense of identity and interact with one another on a sustained basis.
Bias	A bias is a prejudice in a general or specific sense, usually in the sense for having a preference to one particular point of view or ideological perspective.
Social change	Social change refers to alteration in social structures or culture over time.
Attitude	Attitude refers to an enduring mental representation of a person, place, or thing that evokes an emotional response and related behavior.
Femininity	Femininity comprises the physical and mental attributes associated with the female sex and is partly culturally determined.
Society	A society is a grouping of individuals, which is characterized by common interest and may have distinctive culture and institutions.
Acquisition	The initial learning of the stimulus response link, which involves a neutral stimulus being associated with a UCS and becoming a conditioned stimulus, is referred to as an acquisition.
Reliability	Reliability refers to the degree to which a measurement instrument gives the same results with repeated measurements.
Sexual division of labor	The assignment of different work tasks to men and women is called sexual division of labor.
Division of labor	Division of labor is the specialisation of cooperative labor in specific, circumscribed tasks and roles, intended to increase efficiency of output.

Social class	A category of people who occupy a similar position in relation to the means through which goods and services are produced in a society is a social class.
Sexual orientation	Sexual orientation describes the direction of an individual's sexuality, often in relation to their own sex or gender. Common terms for describing sexual orientation include bisexual (bi), heterosexual (straight) and homosexual (lesbian/gay).
Motive	Motive refers to a hypothetical state within an organism that propels the organism toward a goal. In criminal law a motive is the cause that moves people and induce a certain action.
Reinforcement	A stimulus that follows a response and increases the frequency of the response is a reinforcement.
Punishment	Punishment is the practice of imposing something unpleasant on a subject as a response to some unwanted behavior or disobedience that the subject has displayed.
Social learning theory	A theory emphasizing that boys develop maleness and girls develop femaleness through exposure to scores of influence-including parents, peers, television, and schools-that teach them what it means to be a man or a woman in their culture, is referred to as a social learning theory.
Variable	A characteristic that varies in value or magnitude along which an object, individual or group may be categorized, such as income or age, is referred to as a variable.
Adolescence	Adolescence is the transitional stage of human development in which a juvenile matures into an adult. This transition involves biological (i.e. pubertal), social, and psychological changes, though the biological ones are the easiest to measure objectively.
Working class	Working class refers to a social class of industrial societies broadly composed of people involved in manual occupation.
Social institution	Social institution is a group of social positions, connected by social relations, performing a social role. It can be also defined in a narrow sense as any institution in a society that works to socialize the groups or people in it.
Polarization	Polarization, in social psychology, refers to the process by which public opinion divides and goes to the extremes.
Consciousness	The awareness of the senzations, thoughts, and feelings being experienced at a given moment is referred to as consciousness.
Cultural transmission	Cultural transmission refers to the socialization process whereby the norms and values of the group are passed on through learning from one generation to the next generation.
Social reproduction	Social reproduction refers to the processes which perpetuate characteristics of social structure over periods of time.
Bisexual	Bisexual is the sexual orientation which refers to the aesthetic, romantic, or sexual desire for individuals of either gender or of either sex.
Social group	A group that consists of two or more people who interact frequently and share a common identity and a feeling of interdependence, is referred to as a social group.
Dominance	In animal colonies, a condition established by one animal over another by prevailing in an aggressive encounter between the two, is referred to as dominance.
Social role	A social role is a set of connected behaviors, rights and obligations as conceptualized by actors in a social situation. It is mostly defined as an expected behavior in a given individual social status and social position.
Stereotyping	Stereotyping refers to a process whereby a trait, usually negative, is generalized to all members of a particular group.

Labeling	Labeling is defining or describing a person in terms of his or her behavior. The term is often used in sociology to describe human interaction, control and identification of deviant behavior.
Racism	Racism is a belief in the moral or biological superiority of one race or ethnic group over another or others.
Gender role	A gender role is a set of behavioral norms associated with males and with females, respectively, in a given social group or system.
Range	A measure of variability defined as the high score in a distribution minus the low score is referred to as a range.
Agents of Socialization	Those persons, groups, or institutions that teach people what they need to know in order to participate in society are referred to as agents of socialization.

Social position	The social identity an individual has in a given group or society, where social positions may be general in nature or may be more specific, is referred to as a social position.
Society	A society is a grouping of individuals, which is characterized by common interest and may have distinctive culture and institutions.
Hidden curriculum	Behavior or attitudes that are learned at school but which are not a part of the formal curriculum are referred to as hidden curriculum.
Gender	Gender refers to socially defined behavior regarded as appropriate for the members of each
Mass education	Mass education refers to a state-run educational system, usually free and compulsory, that aims to ensure that all children in society have at least a basic education.
Alcoholism	Alcoholism refers to a disorder that involves long-term, repeated, uncontrolled, compulsive, and excessive use of alcoholic beverages and that impairs the drinker's health, work and social relationships.
Juvenile delinquency	Juvenile delinquency refers to antisocial or criminal acts performed by minors. It is an important social issue because juveniles are capable of committing serious crimes, but most legal systems prescribe specific procedures and punishments for dealing with such crimes.
Feminist movement	The collective activities of individuals, groups, and organizations whose goal is the fair and equal treatment of women and men around the world is a feminist movement. They campaign on issues such as reproductive rights (including abortion), domestic violence, maternity leave, equal pay, sexual harassment, and sexual violence.
Depression	In the field of psychiatry, the word depression can also have this meaning of low mood but more specifically refers to a mental illness when it has reached a severity and duration to warrant a diagnosis, whether there is an obvious situational cause or not.
Ideology	Ideology refers to shared ideas or beliefs which serve to justify and support the interests of a particular group or organizations.
Femininity	Femininity comprises the physical and mental attributes associated with the female sex and is partly culturally determined.
Sexism	Sexism is commonly considered to be discrimination and/or hatred against people based on their sex rather than their individual merits, but can also refer to any and all systemic differentiations based on the sex of the individuals.
Racism	Racism is a belief in the moral or biological superiority of one race or ethnic group over another or others.
Civil rights	Civil rights are the protections and privileges of personal liberty given to all citizens by law. Civil rights are rights that are bestowed by nations on those within their territorial boundaries.
Discrimination	Discrimination refers to the denial of equal access to social resources to people on the basis of their group membership.
Frequency	In statistics the frequency of an event i is the number n_i of times the event occurred in the experiment or the study.
Compliance	Conforming behavior that occurs in response to direct social pressure is referred to as compliance.
Standardized test	An oral or written assessment for which an individual receives a score indicating how the individual responded relative to others is a standardized test.
Bias	A bias is a prejudice in a general or specific sense, usually in the sense for having a preference to one particular point of view or ideological perspective.

Prejudice	Prejudice is, as the name implies, the process of "pre-judging" something. It implies coming to a judgment on a subject before learning where the preponderance of evidence actually lies, or forming a judgment without direct experience.
Socialization	Socialization refers to the lifelong processes through which humans develop an awareness of social norms and values, and achieve a distinct sense of self.
Norm	In sociology, a norm, or social norm, is a rule that is socially enforced. Social sanctioning is what distinguishes norms from other cultural products such as meaning and values.
Social class	A category of people who occupy a similar position in relation to the means through which goods and services are produced in a society is a social class.
Reinforcement	A stimulus that follows a response and increases the frequency of the response is a reinforcement.
Content analysis	Content analysis refers to analysis of words and images contained in written, spoken, and visual media.
Slavery	Slavery refers to an extreme form of stratification in which some people are owned by others.
Sexual orientation	Sexual orientation describes the direction of an individual's sexuality, often in relation to their own sex or gender. Common terms for describing sexual orientation include bisexual (bi), heterosexual (straight) and homosexual (lesbian/gay).
Organization	In sociology organization is understood as planned, coordinated and purposeful action of human beings to construct or compile a common tangible or intangible product or service.
Stereotype	A stereotype refers to widely shared beliefs about the characteristic traits, attitudes, and behaviors of members of various social groups, including the assumption that the members of such groups are usually all alike.
Cooperative learning	Cooperative learning was proposed in response to traditional curriculum-driven education. In cooperative learning environments, students interact in purposely structured heterogeneous group to support the learning of one self and others in the same group.
Interdependence	Interdependence is a dynamic of being mutually responsible to and sharing a common set of principles with others. This concept differs dinstinctly from "dependence" in that an interdependent relationship implies that all participants are emotionally, economically, and/or morally "independent."
Mainstreaming	Educating mentally retarded students in regular rather than special schools by placing them in regular classes for part of the day or having special classrooms in regular schools, is referred to as a mainstreaming.
Census	A census is the process of obtaining information about every member of a population. It can be contrasted with sampling in which information is only obtained from a subset of a population. As such it is a method used for accumulating statistical data, and it is also vital to democracy.
Achievement Test	A test designed to determine a person's level of knowledge in a given subject and designed to test what a person has learned or the skills that a person has mastered is referred to as an achievement test.
Adolescence	Adolescence is the transitional stage of human development in which a juvenile matures into an adult. This transition involves biological (i.e. pubertal), social, and psychological changes, though the biological ones are the easiest to measure objectively.
Prestige	Prestige refers to social respect accorded to an individual or group because of the status of their position.

Go to **Cram101.com** for the Practice Tests for this Chapter.

Self-efficacy	Self-efficacy is the belief that one has the capabilities to execute the courses of actions required to manage prospective situations. Unlike efficacy, which is the power to produce an effect (in essence, competence), self-efficacy is the belief (whether or not accurate) that one has the power to produce that effect.
Glass ceiling	Glass ceiling refers to barriers based on attitudinal or organizational bias that prevent qualified females from advancing to top-level positions.
Attribution	Attribution is also a psychological concept. When people watch the world, they do not see it as a completely random stream of happenings, but tend to attribute meanings to things. So, for example when you see someone fall over, you can attribute this to a stable trait, or to a feature of the situation, or to random chance.
Attitude	Attitude refers to an enduring mental representation of a person, place, or thing that evokes an emotional response and related behavior.
Technology	The application of logic, reason and knowledge to the problems of exploiting raw materials from the environment, is referred to as a technology.
Statistics	Statistics is a mathematical science pertaining to the collection, analysis, interpretation, and presentation of data. It is applicable to a wide variety of academic disciplines, from the physical and social sciences to the humanities; it is also used and misused for making informed decisions in all areas of business and government.
Affirmative action	Government programs intended to assure minorities and women equal hiring or admission opportunities is referred to as affirmative action.
Community	Community refers to a group of people who share a common sense of identity and interact with one another on a sustained basis.
Ethnic group	An ethnic group is a human population whose members identify with each other, usually on the basis of a presumed common genealogy or ancestry.
Sexual harassment	Sexual harassment refers to the making of persistent unwanted sexual advances by one individual towards another.
Variable	A characteristic that varies in value or magnitude along which an object, individual or group may be categorized, such as income or age, is referred to as a variable.
Rape	Rape is the act of forcing penetrative sexual acts, against another's will through violence, force, threat of injury, or other duress, or where the victim is unable to decline, due to the effects of drugs or alcohol.
Authority	Authority refers to power that is attached to a position that others perceive as legitimate.
Sanction	A punishment for nonconformity that reinforces socially approved forms of behavior is a sanction.
Social institution	Social institution is a group of social positions, connected by social relations, performing a social role. It can be also defined in a narrow sense as any institution in a society that works to socialize the groups or people in it.
Decenter	Decenter refers to think about more than one characteristic of a thing at a time. A capacity of concrete operational children.
Disability	A physical or health condition that stigmatizes or causes discrimination, is referred to as a disability.
Critical thinking	Critical thinking is an approach to thinking characterized by skepticism and thoughtful analysis of statements and arguments.
Autonomy	Autonomy is a concept found in moral, political, and bioethical philosophy. Within these

contexts it refers to the capacity of a rational individual to make an informed, uncoerced decision. In moral and political philosophy, autonomy is often used as the basis for determining moral responsibility for one's actions.

Social change   Social change refers to alteration in social structures or culture over time.

Status quo   Status quo is a Latin term meaning the present, current, existing state of affairs. To maintain the status quo is to keep things the way they presently are.

Census	A census is the process of obtaining information about every member of a population. It can be contrasted with sampling in which information is only obtained from a subset of a population. As such it is a method used for accumulating statistical data, and it is also vital to democracy.
Mass media	Mass media refers to forms of communication designed to reach a vast audience without any personal contact between the senders and receivers.
Norm	In sociology, a norm, or social norm, is a rule that is socially enforced. Social sanctioning is what distinguishes norms from other cultural products such as meaning and values.
Gender	Gender refers to socially defined behavior regarded as appropriate for the members of each
Society	A society is a grouping of individuals, which is characterized by common interest and may have distinctive culture and institutions.
Socialization	Socialization refers to the lifelong processes through which humans develop an awareness of social norms and values, and achieve a distinct sense of self.
Gender socialization	Gender socialization refers to the aspect of socialization that contains specific messages and practices concerning the nature of being female or male in a specific group or society.
Authority	Authority refers to power that is attached to a position that others perceive as legitimate.
Stereotype	A stereotype refers to widely shared beliefs about the characteristic traits, attitudes, and behaviors of members of various social groups, including the assumption that the members of such groups are usually all alike.
Ageism	Ageism refers to prejudice against a person on the grounds of age in the belief that the age category is inferior to other age categories and that unequal treatment is therefore justified.
Sexism	Sexism is commonly considered to be discrimination and/or hatred against people based on their sex rather than their individual merits, but can also refer to any and all systemic differentiations based on the sex of the individuals.
Community	Community refers to a group of people who share a common sense of identity and interact with one another on a sustained basis.
Social status	Social status refers to a position in a social relationship, a characteristic that locates individuals in relation to other people and sets of role expectations.
Nonverbal communication	Nonverbal communication is usually understood as the process of sending and receiving wordless messages. Such messages can be communicated through gesture; body language or posture; facial expression and eye contact.
Public opinion	Public opinion is the aggregate of individual attitudes or beliefs held by the adult population.
Variable	A characteristic that varies in value or magnitude along which an object, individual or group may be categorized, such as income or age, is referred to as a variable.
Social class	A category of people who occupy a similar position in relation to the means through which goods and services are produced in a society is a social class.
Sexual orientation	Sexual orientation describes the direction of an individual's sexuality, often in relation to their own sex or gender. Common terms for describing sexual orientation include bisexual (bi), heterosexual (straight) and homosexual (lesbian/gay).
Marital status	A person's marital status describes their relationship with a significant other. Some common statuses are: married, single, separated, divorced, widowed, engaged, invalid, annulled, living common-law. The number of children may also be specified and, in this case,

Go to **Cram101.com** for the Practice Tests for this Chapter.
And, **NEVER** highlight a book again!

	becomes synonymous with family status. For example: married with no children. Marital status is often a question on censuses, credit card applications, and many different polls.
Trivialization	A technique for reducing dissonance by mentally minimalizing the importance of attitudes or behavior that are inconsistent with each other, is referred to as trivialization.
Bias	A bias is a prejudice in a general or specific sense, usually in the sense for having a preference to one particular point of view or ideological perspective.
Racism	Racism is a belief in the moral or biological superiority of one race or ethnic group over another or others.
Homophobia	Homophobia is the fear of, aversion to, or discrimination against homosexuality or homosexuals. It can also mean hatred, hostility, or disapproval of homosexual people, sexual behavior, or cultures, and is generally used to assert bigotry.
Attitude	Attitude refers to an enduring mental representation of a person, place, or thing that evokes an emotional response and related behavior.
Cosmopolitan	The word cosmopolitan describes an environment where many cultures from around the world coexist; or a person whose perspective reflects exposure to a variety of cultures. It may also have the weaker senses of "worldly" or "sophisticated".
Femininity	Femininity comprises the physical and mental attributes associated with the female sex and is partly culturally determined.
Range	A measure of variability defined as the high score in a distribution minus the low score is referred to as a range.
Reconstruction	Reconstruction refers to a memory that is not an exact replica of an event but has been pieced together from a few highlights, using information that may or may not be accurate.
Taboo	A taboo is a strong social prohibition (or ban) relating to any area of human activity or social custom declared as sacred and forbidden; breaking of the taboo is usually considered objectionable or abhorrent by society.
Antidepressant	An antidepressant is a medication designed to treat or alleviate the symptoms of clinical depression. Some, notably the tricyclics, are commonly used off-label in the treatment of neuropathic pain, whether or not the patient is depressed. Smaller doses are generally used for this purpose, and they often take effect more quickly.
Masculinity	Masculinity refers to the characteristic forms of behavior expected of men in any given culture.
Incest	Incest is sexual activity between close family members. Incest is considered taboo, and forbidden (fully or slightly) in the majority of current cultures.
Feminism	Feminism is a diverse collection of social theories, political movements and moral philosophies, largely motivated by or concerned with the experiences of women.
Double standard	A double standard is a standard applied more leniently to one group than to another. A double standard violates this principle by holding different people accountable according to different standards.
Stereotyping	Stereotyping refers to a process whereby a trait, usually negative, is generalized to all members of a particular group.
Frequency	In statistics the frequency of an event i is the number n_i of times the event occurred in the experiment or the study.
Rape	Rape is the act of forcing penetrative sexual acts, against another's will through violence, force, threat of injury, or other duress, or where the victim is unable to decline, due to

the effects of drugs or alcohol.

Prejudice

Prejudice is, as the name implies, the process of "pre-judging" something. It implies coming to a judgment on a subject before learning where the preponderance of evidence actually lies, or forming a judgment without direct experience.

Go to **Cram101.com** for the Practice Tests for this Chapter.

Society	A society is a grouping of individuals, which is characterized by common interest and may have distinctive culture and institutions.
Government	A government is a body that has the authority to make and the power to enforce laws within a civil, corporate, religious, academic, or other organization or group.
Domestic violence	Domestic violence occurs when a family member, partner or ex-partner attempts to physically or psychologically dominate or harm the other.
Social problem	A social condition that is perceived as having harmful effects is a social problem. Opinions about whether a condition is a social problem vary among groups and depend upon how and by whom the condition is defined and perceived in society.
Gender	Gender refers to socially defined behavior regarded as appropriate for the members of each
Norm	In sociology, a norm, or social norm, is a rule that is socially enforced. Social sanctioning is what distinguishes norms from other cultural products such as meaning and values.
Relations of production	Relations of production is a concept frequently used by Karl Marx in his theory of historical materialism and in Das Kapital. Beyond examining specific cases, Marx never defined the general concept exactly however. It is evident though that it refers to all kinds of social and technical human interconnections involved in the social production and reproduction of material life.
Social construction	A social construction is an institutionalized entity or artifact in a social system 'invented' or 'constructed' by participants in a particular culture or society that exists solely because people agree to behave as if it exists, or agree to follow certain conventional rules.
Nuclear family	The term nuclear family was developed in the western world to distinguish the family group consisting of parents and their children, usually a father, mother, and children, from what is known as an extended family.
Primary socialization	Primary socialization is the process whereby people learn the attitudes, values, and actions appropriate to individuals as members of a particular culture.
Socialization	Socialization refers to the lifelong processes through which humans develop an awareness of social norms and values, and achieve a distinct sense of self.
Gender role	A gender role is a set of behavioral norms associated with males and with females, respectively, in a given social group or system.
Life expectancy	The number of years a newborn in a particular society can expect to live is referred to as a life expectancy.
Working class	Working class refers to a social class of industrial societies broadly composed of people involved in manual occupation.
Division of labor	Division of labor is the specialisation of cooperative labor in specific, circumscribed tasks and roles, intended to increase efficiency of output.
Census	A census is the process of obtaining information about every member of a population. It can be contrasted with sampling in which information is only obtained from a subset of a population. As such it is a method used for accumulating statistical data, and it is also vital to democracy.
Homophobia	Homophobia is the fear of, aversion to, or discrimination against homosexuality or homosexuals. It can also mean hatred, hostility, or disapproval of homosexual people, sexual behavior, or cultures, and is generally used to assert bigotry.
Sexual	Sexual orientation describes the direction of an individual's sexuality, often in relation

orientation	to their own sex or gender. Common terms for describing sexual orientation include bisexual (bi), heterosexual (straight) and homosexual (lesbian/gay).
Kinship	Kinship is the most basic principle of organizing individuals into social groups, roles, and categories. It was originally thought to be determined by biological descent, a view that was challenged by David M. Schneider in his work on Symbolic Kinship.
Sexually transmitted disease	Disease transmitted through sexual contact is a sexually transmitted disease.
Attitude	Attitude refers to an enduring mental representation of a person, place, or thing that evokes an emotional response and related behavior.
Sexual double standard	The belief that men have exclusive rights of erotic access to women without women possessing reciprocal exclusive rights of erotic access to men is a sexual double standard.
Double standard	A double standard is a standard applied more leniently to one group than to another. A double standard violates this principle by holding different people accountable according to different standards.
Prejudice	Prejudice is, as the name implies, the process of "pre-judging" something. It implies coming to a judgment on a subject before learning where the preponderance of evidence actually lies, or forming a judgment without direct experience.
Public opinion	Public opinion is the aggregate of individual attitudes or beliefs held by the adult population.
Range	A measure of variability defined as the high score in a distribution minus the low score is referred to as a range.
Coalition	A coalition is an alliance among entities, during which they cooperate in joint action, each in their own self-interest. This alliance may be temporary or a matter of convenience.
Abortion	An abortion is the removal or expulsion of an embryo or fetus from the uterus, resulting in, or caused by, its death. This can occur spontaneously as a miscarriage, or be artificially induced through chemical, surgical or other means. Commonly, " abortion " refers to an induced procedure at any point in the pregnancy; medically, it is defined as a miscarriage or induced termination before twenty weeks gestation, which is considered nonviable.
Birth control	Birth control is a regimen of one or more actions, devices, or medications followed in order to deliberately prevent or reduce the likelihood of a woman giving birth or becoming pregnant.
Authority	Authority refers to power that is attached to a position that others perceive as legitimate.
Technology	The application of logic, reason and knowledge to the problems of exploiting raw materials from the environment, is referred to as a technology.
Reproductive technology	Procedures that bypass sexual intercourse to conceive babies are described as reproductive technology, such as in vitro fertilization and artificial insemination.
Social class	A category of people who occupy a similar position in relation to the means through which goods and services are produced in a society is a social class.
Variable	A characteristic that varies in value or magnitude along which an object, individual or group may be categorized, such as income or age, is referred to as a variable.
Ideology	Ideology refers to shared ideas or beliefs which serve to justify and support the interests of a particular group or organizations.
Autonomy	Autonomy is a concept found in moral, political, and bioethical philosophy. Within these

contexts it refers to the capacity of a rational individual to make an informed, uncoerced decision. In moral and political philosophy, autonomy is often used as the basis for determining moral responsibility for one's actions.

Community	Community refers to a group of people who share a common sense of identity and interact with one another on a sustained basis.
Joint custody	Joint custody refers to legal award of responsibility for residence, care, and control of a child to both parents jointly after a separation or divorce.
Joint legal custody	Custody shared by both parents, both of whom are responsible for child rearing and for making decisions regarding the child, is referred to as joint legal custody.
Joint physical custody	Legal award following divorce in which child resides approximately equally with each parent for alternating time periods is called joint physical custody.
Physical custody	Physical custody involves the day-to-day care of a child and establishes where a child will live. The parent with physical custody has the right to have his/her child live with him/her.
Median	The number that falls halfway in a range of numbers, or the score below which are half the scores and above which are the other half is a median.
No-fault divorce	A legal approach that eliminates fault as a precondition for access to courts and recognizes the right of individuals to petition for divorce on the grounds of irretrievable breakdown of the marriage or irreconcilable differences, is referred to as a no-fault divorce.
Child support	Income paid to a former spouse for support of dependent children following a divorce or separation is child support.
Feminization of poverty	The feminization of poverty has been observed since 1970 as female headed households accounted for a growing proportion of those below the poverty line. A large majority of these women are divorced or never-married mothers.
Alcoholism	Alcoholism refers to a disorder that involves long-term, repeated, uncontrolled, compulsive, and excessive use of alcoholic beverages and that impairs the drinker's health, work and social relationships.
Aggregate	Aggregate refers to a collection of people who happen to be in the same place at the same time.
Depression	In the field of psychiatry, the word depression can also have this meaning of low mood but more specifically refers to a mental illness when it has reached a severity and duration to warrant a diagnosis, whether there is an obvious situational cause or not.
Domestic partnership	A household partnership in which an unmarried couple lives together in a committed, sexually intimate relationship and is granted the same benefits as those accorded to married heterosexual couples is a domestic partnership.
Stereotype	A stereotype refers to widely shared beliefs about the characteristic traits, attitudes, and behaviors of members of various social groups, including the assumption that the members of such groups are usually all alike.
Socioeconomic status	An overall rank based on characteristics such as education and occupation, used to describe people's positions in stratification systems is referred to as socioeconomic status.
Mortality rate	Mortality rate is a measure of the number of deaths in some population, scaled to the size of that population, per unit time. Mortality rate is typically expressed in units of deaths per 1000 individuals per year; thus, a mortality rate of 10000.5 in a population of 100,000 would mean 1,000,500 deaths per year in the entire population.
Statistics	Statistics is a mathematical science pertaining to the collection, analysis, interpretation,

and presentation of data. It is applicable to a wide variety of academic disciplines, from the physical and social sciences to the humanities; it is also used and misused for making informed decisions in all areas of business and government.

Cohabitation	Cohabitation refers to living together in a sexual relationship of some permanence without being legally married.
Egalitarianism	Egalitarianism is any belief that emphasizes some form of equality between morally-significant beings (usually meaning humans, but sometimes expanded to include certain animals as well).
Monogamy	Monogamy is the custom or condition of having only one mate during a period of time.
Discrimination	Discrimination refers to the denial of equal access to social resources to people on the basis of their group membership.
Affinity	Affinity in terms of sociology, refers to "kinship of spirit", interest and other interpersonal commonalities. Affinity is characterized by high levels of intimacy and sharing.
Child abuse	Child abuse refers to not only physical assaults on a child but also malnourishment, abandonment, neglect, emotional abuse and sexual abuse.
Elder abuse	Elder abuse refers to a term used to describe physical abuse, psychological abuse, financial exploitation, and medical abuse or neglect of people age 65 or older.
Frequency	In statistics the frequency of an event i is the number n_i of times the event occurred in the experiment or the study.
Random sample	A sample is a subset chosen from a population for investigation. A random sample is one chosen by a method involving an unpredictable component.
Substance abuse	Substance abuse refers to the overindulgence in and dependence on a psychoactive leading to effects that are detrimental to the individual's physical health or mental health, or the welfare of others.
Probation	Nonpunitive, legal disposition of juveniles emphasizing community treatment in which the juvenile is closely supervized by an officer of the court and must adhere to a strict set of rules to avoid incarceration is probation.
Child maltreatment	Child abuse is the physical or psychological maltreatment of a child by an adult often synonymous with the term child maltreatment or the term child abuse and neglect.
Adolescence	Adolescence is the transitional stage of human development in which a juvenile matures into an adult. This transition involves biological (i.e. pubertal), social, and psychological changes, though the biological ones are the easiest to measure objectively.
Mood disorder	A mood disorder is a condition whereby the prevailing emotional mood is distorted or inappropriate to the circumstances.
Social isolation	A type of loneliness that occurs when a person lacks a sense of integrated involvement. Being deprived of participation in a group or community involving companionship, shared interests, organized activities, and meaningful roles causes a person to feel is a social isolation.
Punishment	Punishment is the practice of imposing something unpleasant on a subject as a response to some unwanted behavior or disobedience that the subject has displayed.
Racism	Racism is a belief in the moral or biological superiority of one race or ethnic group over another or others.
Ageism	Ageism refers to prejudice against a person on the grounds of age in the belief that the age category is inferior to other age categories and that unequal treatment is therefore

	justified.
Social institution	Social institution is a group of social positions, connected by social relations, performing a social role. It can be also defined in a narrow sense as any institution in a society that works to socialize the groups or people in it.

47

Organization	In sociology organization is understood as planned, coordinated and purposeful action of human beings to construct or compile a common tangible or intangible product or service.
Society	A society is a grouping of individuals, which is characterized by common interest and may have distinctive culture and institutions.
Labor force	Normally, the labor force consists of everyone of working age (typically above a certain age (around 14 to 16) and below retirement (around 65) who are participating workers, that is people actively employed or seeking employment.
Gender	Gender refers to socially defined behavior regarded as appropriate for the members of each
Ideology	Ideology refers to shared ideas or beliefs which serve to justify and support the interests of a particular group or organizations.
Working class	Working class refers to a social class of industrial societies broadly composed of people involved in manual occupation.
Stereotype	A stereotype refers to widely shared beliefs about the characteristic traits, attitudes, and behaviors of members of various social groups, including the assumption that the members of such groups are usually all alike.
Tolerance	Tolerance is a recent political term used within debates in areas of social, cultural and religious context, as an emphatic antithesis to discrimination, as such may advocate persecution. Its usage came about as a more widely acceptable alternative to "acceptance", the usage of which had been widely derided, as certain cases would not be considered by common society as acceptable.
Discrimination	Discrimination refers to the denial of equal access to social resources to people on the basis of their group membership.
Social disorganization	Social disorganization refers to a structural condition of society caused by rapid change in social institutions, norms, and values.
Urbanization	Urbanization is the increase over time in the population of cities in relation to the region's rural population. Urbanization has intense effects on the ecology of a region and on its economy.
Immigration	Although human migration has existed for hundreds of thousands of years, immigration in the modern sense refers to movement of people from one nation-state to another, where they are not citizens.
Statistics	Statistics is a mathematical science pertaining to the collection, analysis, interpretation, and presentation of data. It is applicable to a wide variety of academic disciplines, from the physical and social sciences to the humanities; it is also used and misused for making informed decisions in all areas of business and government.
Depression	In the field of psychiatry, the word depression can also have this meaning of low mood but more specifically refers to a mental illness when it has reached a severity and duration to warrant a diagnosis, whether there is an obvious situational cause or not.
Norm	In sociology, a norm, or social norm, is a rule that is socially enforced. Social sanctioning is what distinguishes norms from other cultural products such as meaning and values.
Government	A government is a body that has the authority to make and the power to enforce laws within a civil, corporate, religious, academic, or other organization or group.
Propaganda	Information provided by individuals or groups that have a vested interest in furthering their own cause or damaging an opposing one, is referred to as propaganda.
Public opinion	Public opinion is the aggregate of individual attitudes or beliefs held by the adult

	population.
Sector	Sector refers to parts of the economy as judged by the economic activity that they constitute. For example agriculture, forestry, fishing and mining constitute the primary sector.
Life expectancy	The number of years a newborn in a particular society can expect to live is referred to as a life expectancy.
Fertility rate	The average number of children a woman can expect to have over her life, based on current rates of child-bearing is a fertility rate.
Divorce rate	The number of divorces over a specified period per specified popularion. The divorce rate is often calculated per 1,000 population or by estimating the proportion of all marriages that are expected to end in divorce.
Census	A census is the process of obtaining information about every member of a population. It can be contrasted with sampling in which information is only obtained from a subset of a population. As such it is a method used for accumulating statistical data, and it is also vital to democracy.
Feminist movement	The collective activities of individuals, groups, and organizations whose goal is the fair and equal treatment of women and men around the world is a feminist movement. They campaign on issues such as reproductive rights (including abortion), domestic violence, maternity leave, equal pay, sexual harassment, and sexual violence.
Technology	The application of logic, reason and knowledge to the problems of exploiting raw materials from the environment, is referred to as a technology.
Variable	A characteristic that varies in value or magnitude along which an object, individual or group may be categorized, such as income or age, is referred to as a variable.
Dominance	In animal colonies, a condition established by one animal over another by prevailing in an aggressive encounter between the two, is referred to as dominance.
Prestige	Prestige refers to social respect accorded to an individual or group because of the status of their position.
Professional-zation	The social process through which an occupation acquires the cultural and structural characteristics of a profession is professionalization.
Affirmative action	Government programs intended to assure minorities and women equal hiring or admission opportunities is referred to as affirmative action.
Autonomy	Autonomy is a concept found in moral, political, and bioethical philosophy. Within these contexts it refers to the capacity of a rational individual to make an informed, uncoerced decision. In moral and political philosophy, autonomy is often used as the basis for determining moral responsibility for one's actions.
Tokenism	Tokenism refers to a policy or practice of limited inclusion of members of a minority group, usually creating a false appearance of inclusive practices, intentional or not. Typical examples in real life and fiction include purposely including a member of a minority race (such as a black character in a mainly white cast, or vice versa) into a group.
Social network	A social network is a social structure made of nodes which are generally individuals or organizations. It indicates the ways in which they are connected through various social familiarities ranging from casual acquaintance to close familial bonds.
Social status	Social status refers to a position in a social relationship, a characteristic that locates individuals in relation to other people and sets of role expectations.

Glass ceiling	Glass ceiling refers to barriers based on attitudinal or organizational bias that prevent qualified females from advancing to top-level positions.
Glass escalator	The term glass elevator or glass escalator is used to describe the rapid promotion of men over women, especially into management, in female-dominated fields like nursing.
Attitude	Attitude refers to an enduring mental representation of a person, place, or thing that evokes an emotional response and related behavior.
Masculinity	Masculinity refers to the characteristic forms of behavior expected of men in any given culture.
Prejudice	Prejudice is, as the name implies, the process of "pre-judging" something. It implies coming to a judgment on a subject before learning where the preponderance of evidence actually lies, or forming a judgment without direct experience.
Authority	Authority refers to power that is attached to a position that others perceive as legitimate.
Sexual harassment	Sexual harassment refers to the making of persistent unwanted sexual advances by one individual towards another.
Wage gap	Income disparity or wage gap is a term used to describe inequities in average pay or salary between socio-economic groups within society, or the inequities in pay between individuals who produce the same work. Income disparity generally occurs when certain groups within society suffer from social inequality within a society.
Median	The number that falls halfway in a range of numbers, or the score below which are half the scores and above which are the other half is a median.
Educational attainment	Educational attainment is a term commonly used by statisticans to refer to the highest degree of education an individual has completed.
Disability	A physical or health condition that stigmatizes or causes discrimination, is referred to as a disability.
Poverty line	The poverty threshold, or poverty line, is the level of income below which one cannot afford to purchase all the resources one requires to live. Thus, by definition, nobody lives below the poverty line.
Participant observation	Participant observation is a major research strategy which aims to gain a close and intimate familiarity with a given group of individuals (such as a religious, occupational, or deviant group) and their practices through an intensive involvement with people in their natural environment.
Working poor	Working poor is a term used to describe individuals and families who maintain regular employment but remain in relative poverty due to low levels of pay and dependent expenses.
Child support	Income paid to a former spouse for support of dependent children following a divorce or separation is child support.
Sexism	Sexism is commonly considered to be discrimination and/or hatred against people based on their sex rather than their individual merits, but can also refer to any and all systemic differentiations based on the sex of the individuals.
Racism	Racism is a belief in the moral or biological superiority of one race or ethnic group over another or others.
Range	A measure of variability defined as the high score in a distribution minus the low score is referred to as a range.
Acquisition	The initial learning of the stimulus response link, which involves a neutral stimulus being associated with a UCS and becoming a conditioned stimulus, is referred to as an acquisition.

53

Human capital theory	Argument that individuals make investments in their own human capital through training and education in order to increase their productivity and earnings, is referred to as the human capital theory.
Human capital	Human capital is a way of defining and categorizing peoples' skills and abilities as used in employment and as they otherwise contribute to the economy. Many early economic theories refer to it simply as labor, one of three factors of production, and consider it to be a commodity.
Stereotyping	Stereotyping refers to a process whereby a trait, usually negative, is generalized to all members of a particular group.
Civil rights	Civil rights are the protections and privileges of personal liberty given to all citizens by law. Civil rights are rights that are bestowed by nations on those within their territorial boundaries.
Compliance	Conforming behavior that occurs in response to direct social pressure is referred to as compliance.
Comparable worth	The evaluation of jobs dominated by women and those traditionally dominated by men on the basis of training, skills, and experience in attempts to equalize wage is referred to as comparable worth.

Civil rights	Civil rights are the protections and privileges of personal liberty given to all citizens by law. Civil rights are rights that are bestowed by nations on those within their territorial boundaries.
Civil law	A norm that regulates social relationships in order to prevent or undo the negative effects of particular acts is a civil law.
Gender	Gender refers to socially defined behavior regarded as appropriate for the members of each
Criminal law	Criminal law (also known as penal law) is the body of statutory and common law that deals with crime and the legal punishment of criminal offenses. There are four theories of criminal justice: punishment, deterrence, incapacitation, and rehabilitation.
Society	A society is a grouping of individuals, which is characterized by common interest and may have distinctive culture and institutions.
Criminal justice	Criminal justice refers to the system used by government to maintain social control, enforce laws, and administer justice. Law enforcement (police), courts, and corrections are the primary agencies charged with these responsibilities.
Social class	A category of people who occupy a similar position in relation to the means through which goods and services are produced in a society is a social class.
Sexual orientation	Sexual orientation describes the direction of an individual's sexuality, often in relation to their own sex or gender. Common terms for describing sexual orientation include bisexual (bi), heterosexual (straight) and homosexual (lesbian/gay).
Crime	Crime refers to any action that violates criminal laws established by political authority. A crime in a nontechnical sense is an act that violates a very important political or moral command.
Crime rate	Crime rate is a measure of the rate of occurrence of crimes committed in a given area and time. Most commonly, crime rate is given as the number of crimes committed among a given number of persons.
Statistics	Statistics is a mathematical science pertaining to the collection, analysis, interpretation, and presentation of data. It is applicable to a wide variety of academic disciplines, from the physical and social sciences to the humanities; it is also used and misused for making informed decisions in all areas of business and government.
Robbery	The unlawful taking of, or the attempt to take something of value from another person or persons by using violence or the threat of violence, is referred to as a robbery.
Embezzlement	Embezzlement is the fraudulent appropriation by a person to his own use of property or money entrusted to that person's care but owned by someone else.
Feminism	Feminism is a diverse collection of social theories, political movements and moral philosophies, largely motivated by or concerned with the experiences of women.
Feminist movement	The collective activities of individuals, groups, and organizations whose goal is the fair and equal treatment of women and men around the world is a feminist movement. They campaign on issues such as reproductive rights (including abortion), domestic violence, maternity leave, equal pay, sexual harassment, and sexual violence.
Unemployment rate	In economics, one who is willing to work at a prevailing wage rate yet is unable to find a paying job is considered to be unemployed. The unemployment rate is the number of unemployed workers divided by the total civilian labor force, which includes both the unemployed and those with jobs (all those willing and able to work for pay).
Aggravated Assault	Aggravated assault refers to an unlawful attack by one person upon another for the purpose of inflicting severe or aggravated bodily injury.

Go to **Cram101.com** for the Practice Tests for this Chapter.

Domestic violence	Domestic violence occurs when a family member, partner or ex-partner attempts to physically or psychologically dominate or harm the other.
Gender role	A gender role is a set of behavioral norms associated with males and with females, respectively, in a given social group or system.
Labor force	Normally, the labor force consists of everyone of working age (typically above a certain age (around 14 to 16) and below retirement (around 65) who are participating workers, that is people actively employed or seeking employment.
Corporate crime	In criminology, corporate crime refers to crimes either committed by a corporation, i.e. a business entity having a separate legal personality from the natural persons that manage its activities, or by individuals that may be identified with a corporation or other business entity.
Insider trading	Insider trading is the trading of a corporation's stock or other securities (e.g. bonds or stock options) by corporate insiders such as officers, directors, or holders of more than ten percent of the firm's shares. Insider trading may be perfectly legal, but the term is frequently used to refer to a practice, illegal in many jurisdictions, in which an insider or a related party trades based on material non-public information obtained during the performance of the insider's duties at the corporation, or otherwise misappropriated.
Government	A government is a body that has the authority to make and the power to enforce laws within a civil, corporate, religious, academic, or other organization or group.
Motive	Motive refers to a hypothetical state within an organism that propels the organism toward a goal. In criminal law a motive is the cause that moves people and induce a certain action.
Shoplifting	Shoplifting (also known as retail theft) is theft of merchandise for sale in a shop, store, or other retail establishment, by an ostensible patron. It is one of the most common crimes for police and courts.
Discrimination	Discrimination refers to the denial of equal access to social resources to people on the basis of their group membership.
Dominance	In animal colonies, a condition established by one animal over another by prevailing in an aggressive encounter between the two, is referred to as dominance.
Masculinity	Masculinity refers to the characteristic forms of behavior expected of men in any given culture.
Sexual harassment	Sexual harassment refers to the making of persistent unwanted sexual advances by one individual towards another.
Attitude	Attitude refers to an enduring mental representation of a person, place, or thing that evokes an emotional response and related behavior.
Community	Community refers to a group of people who share a common sense of identity and interact with one another on a sustained basis.
Community policing	Community policing is a political philosophy in which the police and police department are seen as members of the community, with police officers being part of where they live and work. Cities and counties that subscribe to this philosophy tend to do much more community work than traditional police departments.
Neighborhood	A neighborhood is a geographically localized community located within a larger city, town or suburb. Traditionally, a neighborhood is small enough that the neighbors are all able to know each other.
Stereotyping	Stereotyping refers to a process whereby a trait, usually negative, is generalized to all members of a particular group.

Stereotype	A stereotype refers to widely shared beliefs about the characteristic traits, attitudes, and behaviors of members of various social groups, including the assumption that the members of such groups are usually all alike.
Sexism	Sexism is commonly considered to be discrimination and/or hatred against people based on their sex rather than their individual merits, but can also refer to any and all systemic differentiations based on the sex of the individuals.
Racism	Racism is a belief in the moral or biological superiority of one race or ethnic group over another or others.
Ageism	Ageism refers to prejudice against a person on the grounds of age in the belief that the age category is inferior to other age categories and that unequal treatment is therefore justified.
Femininity	Femininity comprises the physical and mental attributes associated with the female sex and is partly culturally determined.
Authority	Authority refers to power that is attached to a position that others perceive as legitimate.
Affirmative action	Government programs intended to assure minorities and women equal hiring or admission opportunities is referred to as affirmative action.
Bias	A bias is a prejudice in a general or specific sense, usually in the sense for having a preference to one particular point of view or ideological perspective.
Public sector	Public sector refers to that part of a national economy subject to direct government ownership and control. The constituents of the public sector are the departments of central and local government, various government agencies and the nationalized industries.
Sector	Sector refers to parts of the economy as judged by the economic activity that they constitute. For example agriculture, forestry, fishing and mining constitute the primary sector.
Jurisdiction	Jurisdiction refers to every kind of judicial action; the authority of courts and judicial officers to decide cases.
Labeling	Labeling is defining or describing a person in terms of his or her behavior. The term is often used in sociology to describe human interaction, control and identification of deviant behavior.
Marital status	A person's marital status describes their relationship with a significant other. Some common statuses are: married, single, separated, divorced, widowed, engaged, invalid, annulled, living common-law. The number of children may also be specified and, in this case, becomes synonymous with family status. For example: married with no children. Marital status is often a question on censuses, credit card applications, and many different polls.
Conformity	Conformity is the act of consciously maintaining a certain degree of similarity (in clothing, manners, behaviors, etc.) to those in your general social circles, to those in authority, or to the general status quo. Usually, conformity implies a tendency to submit to others in thought and behavior other than simply clothing choice.
Norm	In sociology, a norm, or social norm, is a rule that is socially enforced. Social sanctioning is what distinguishes norms from other cultural products such as meaning and values.
Punishment	Punishment is the practice of imposing something unpleasant on a subject as a response to some unwanted behavior or disobedience that the subject has displayed.
Census	A census is the process of obtaining information about every member of a population. It can be contrasted with sampling in which information is only obtained from a subset of a population. As such it is a method used for accumulating statistical data, and it is also

vital to democracy.

Murder	Murder is the unlawful, premeditated killing of a human being by another. The penalty for murder is usually either life imprisonment, or in jurisdictions with capital punishment, the death penalty.
Variable	A characteristic that varies in value or magnitude along which an object, individual or group may be categorized, such as income or age, is referred to as a variable.
Status offense	A status offense is an action that is a crime only if the perpetrator is a minor. For instance, consumption of alcohol by a minor may be a status offense in jurisdictions where such consumption is permitted, but only by persons over a specified age.
Sexual double standard	The belief that men have exclusive rights of erotic access to women without women possessing reciprocal exclusive rights of erotic access to men is a sexual double standard.
Double standard	A double standard is a standard applied more leniently to one group than to another. A double standard violates this principle by holding different people accountable according to different standards.
Juvenile justice system	The segment of the justice system including law enforcement officers, the courts, and correctional agencies, designed to treat youthful offenders is referred to as the juvenile justice system.
Delinquency prevention	That which involves any nonjustice program or policy designed to prevent the occurrence of a future delinquent act is referred to as delinquency prevention.
Probation	Nonpunitive, legal disposition of juveniles emphasizing community treatment in which the juvenile is closely supervized by an officer of the court and must adhere to a strict set of rules to avoid incarceration is probation.
Detention	Temporary care of a child alleged to be delinquent who requires secure custody in physically restricting facilities pending court disposition or execution of a court order is detention.
Ideology	Ideology refers to shared ideas or beliefs which serve to justify and support the interests of a particular group or organizations.
Depression	In the field of psychiatry, the word depression can also have this meaning of low mood but more specifically refers to a mental illness when it has reached a severity and duration to warrant a diagnosis, whether there is an obvious situational cause or not.
Substance abuse	Substance abuse refers to the overindulgence in and dependence on a psychoactive leading to effects that are detrimental to the individual's physical health or mental health, or the welfare of others.
Addiction	A pattern of behavior characterized by an overwhelming involvement with using a drug and securing its supply is defined as an addiction.
Heroin	A highly addictive, partly synthetic narcotic derived from morphine is heroin. It mimics endorphins and thus causes a high sense of well-being when entered into the bloodstream (usually through injection).
Rape	Rape is the act of forcing penetrative sexual acts, against another's will through violence, force, threat of injury, or other duress, or where the victim is unable to decline, due to the effects of drugs or alcohol.
Range	A measure of variability defined as the high score in a distribution minus the low score is referred to as a range.
Abandonment	Parents that physically leave their children with the intention of completely severing the parent-child relationship are engaging in abandonment.To give up control of a child, legally

terminating parental rights; in many states abandonment is considered child abuse.

Random sample	A sample is a subset chosen from a population for investigation. A random sample is one chosen by a method involving an unpredictable component.
Victimizations	Victimizations refer to the number of people who are victims of criminal acts; young teens are fifteen times more likely than older adults to be victims of crimes.
Technology	The application of logic, reason and knowledge to the problems of exploiting raw materials from the environment, is referred to as a technology.
Victim precipitation	The Victim Precipitation theory was first introduced by Von Hentig in the 1940s: "The victim shapes and molds the criminals."
Date rape	The term, date rape refers to rape or non-consensual sexual activity between people who are already acquainted, or who know each other socially — friends, acquaintances, people on a date, or even people in an existing romantic relationship — where it is alleged that consent for sexual activity was not given, or was given under duress.
Alcoholism	Alcoholism refers to a disorder that involves long-term, repeated, uncontrolled, compulsive, and excessive use of alcoholic beverages and that impairs the drinker's health, work and social relationships.
Addict	A person with an overpowering physical or psychological need to continue taking a particular substance or drug is referred to as an addict.
Social structure	The term social structure, used in a general sense, refers to entities or groups in definite relation to each other, to relatively enduring patterns of behavior and relationship within social systems, or to social institutions and norms becoming embedded into social systems in such a way that they shape the behavior of actors within those social systems.
Industrialized societies	Strongly developed nation-states in which the majority of the population work in factories or offices rather than in agriculture, and most people live in urban areas are referred to as industrialized societies.
Peer group	A friendship group with common interests and position composed of individuals of similar age is referred to as a peer group.
Subculture	A group within the broader society that has values, norms and lifestyle distinct from those of the majority, is referred to as a subculture.
Social network	A social network is a social structure made of nodes which are generally individuals or organizations. It indicates the ways in which they are connected through various social familiarities ranging from casual acquaintance to close familial bonds.
Commodity	Commodity is defined as a good or service produced primarily for its exchange value, not for direct consumption by the producer. In Marx's theory, a commodity has value, which represents a quantity of human labor.
Causal Relationship	A relationship in which one state of affairs is brought about by another is defined as a causal relationship.
Eros	Eros is the life instinct innate in all humans. It is the desire to create life and favors productivity and construction.
Arousal	Arousal is a physiological and psychological state involving the activation of the reticular activating system in the brain stem, the autonomic nervous system and the endocrine system, leading to increased heart rate and blood pressure and a condition of alertness and readiness to respond.
Censorship	The practice of suppressing material that is considered morally, politically, or otherwise

	objectionable is referred to as censorship.
Ritual	A ritual is a set of actions, performed mainly for their symbolic value, which is prescribed by a religion or by the traditions of a community.
Polygamy	A form of marriage in which a person may have more than one spouse simultaneously is polygamy.

66

Go to **Cram101.com** for the Practice Tests for this Chapter.

Society	A society is a grouping of individuals, which is characterized by common interest and may have distinctive culture and institutions.
Gender	Gender refers to socially defined behavior regarded as appropriate for the members of each
Attitude	Attitude refers to an enduring mental representation of a person, place, or thing that evokes an emotional response and related behavior.
Government	A government is a body that has the authority to make and the power to enforce laws within a civil, corporate, religious, academic, or other organization or group.
Educational attainment	Educational attainment is a term commonly used by statisticans to refer to the highest degree of education an individual has completed.
Statistics	Statistics is a mathematical science pertaining to the collection, analysis, interpretation, and presentation of data. It is applicable to a wide variety of academic disciplines, from the physical and social sciences to the humanities; it is also used and misused for making informed decisions in all areas of business and government.
Crime	Crime refers to any action that violates criminal laws established by political authority. A crime in a nontechnical sense is an act that violates a very important political or moral command.
Abortion	An abortion is the removal or expulsion of an embryo or fetus from the uterus, resulting in, or caused by, its death. This can occur spontaneously as a miscarriage, or be artificially induced through chemical, surgical or other means. Commonly, " abortion " refers to an induced procedure at any point in the pregnancy; medically, it is defined as a miscarriage or induced termination before twenty weeks gestation, which is considered nonviable.
Social class	A category of people who occupy a similar position in relation to the means through which goods and services are produced in a society is a social class.
Marital status	A person's marital status describes their relationship with a significant other. Some common statuses are: married, single, separated, divorced, widowed, engaged, invalid, annulled, living common-law. The number of children may also be specified and, in this case, becomes synonymous with family status. For example: married with no children. Marital status is often a question on censuses, credit card applications, and many different polls.
Sexual orientation	Sexual orientation describes the direction of an individual's sexuality, often in relation to their own sex or gender. Common terms for describing sexual orientation include bisexual (bi), heterosexual (straight) and homosexual (lesbian/gay).
Homophobia	Homophobia is the fear of, aversion to, or discrimination against homosexuality or homosexuals. It can also mean hatred, hostility, or disapproval of homosexual people, sexual behavior, or cultures, and is generally used to assert bigotry.
Bisexual	Bisexual is the sexual orientation which refers to the aesthetic, romantic, or sexual desire for individuals of either gender or of either sex.
Transgendered	Transgender is an overarching term applied to a variety of individuals, behaviors, and groups involving tendencies that diverge from the normative gender role (woman or man) commonly, but not always, assigned at birth, as well as the role traditionally held by society.
Community	Community refers to a group of people who share a common sense of identity and interact with one another on a sustained basis.
Stereotype	A stereotype refers to widely shared beliefs about the characteristic traits, attitudes, and behaviors of members of various social groups, including the assumption that the members of such groups are usually all alike.
Dominance	In animal colonies, a condition established by one animal over another by prevailing in an

aggressive encounter between the two, is referred to as dominance.

Affirmative action	Government programs intended to assure minorities and women equal hiring or admission opportunities is referred to as affirmative action.
Socialization	Socialization refers to the lifelong processes through which humans develop an awareness of social norms and values, and achieve a distinct sense of self.
Prejudice	Prejudice is, as the name implies, the process of "pre-judging" something. It implies coming to a judgment on a subject before learning where the preponderance of evidence actually lies, or forming a judgment without direct experience.
Discrimination	Discrimination refers to the denial of equal access to social resources to people on the basis of their group membership.
Sexism	Sexism is commonly considered to be discrimination and/or hatred against people based on their sex rather than their individual merits, but can also refer to any and all systemic differentiations based on the sex of the individuals.
Bias	A bias is a prejudice in a general or specific sense, usually in the sense for having a preference to one particular point of view or ideological perspective.
Census	A census is the process of obtaining information about every member of a population. It can be contrasted with sampling in which information is only obtained from a subset of a population. As such it is a method used for accumulating statistical data, and it is also vital to democracy.
Special interest groups	Political coalitions comprized of individuals or groups that share a specific interest that they wish to protect or advance with the help of the political system is referred to as special interest groups.
Interest group	Interest group refers to an organization that attempts to affect political decisions by supporting candidates sympathetic to their interests and by influencing those already in positions of authority.
Sexual harassment	Sexual harassment refers to the making of persistent unwanted sexual advances by one individual towards another.
Civil rights	Civil rights are the protections and privileges of personal liberty given to all citizens by law. Civil rights are rights that are bestowed by nations on those within their territorial boundaries.
Domestic violence	Domestic violence occurs when a family member, partner or ex-partner attempts to physically or psychologically dominate or harm the other.
Norm	In sociology, a norm, or social norm, is a rule that is socially enforced. Social sanctioning is what distinguishes norms from other cultural products such as meaning and values.
Standing army	A standing army is an army composed of full time professional soldiers. They differ from army reserves who are activated only during such times as war or natural disasters.
Second world	The subjective term Second World, is one of the terms that can be used to divide the nations of Earth into three broad categories. The term Second World has largely fallen out of use because the circumstances to which it referred largely ended with the 1991 collapse of the Soviet Union.
Socialism	Socialism refers to a broad array of doctrines or political movements that envisage a socio-economic system in which property and the distribution of wealth are subject to social control.
Unemployment	In economics, one who is willing to work at a prevailing wage rate yet is unable to find a

rate	paying job is considered to be unemployed. The unemployment rate is the number of unemployed workers divided by the total civilian labor force, which includes both the unemployed and those with jobs (all those willing and able to work for pay).
Racism	Racism is a belief in the moral or biological superiority of one race or ethnic group over another or others.
Motive	Motive refers to a hypothetical state within an organism that propels the organism toward a goal. In criminal law a motive is the cause that moves people and induce a certain action.
Technology	The application of logic, reason and knowledge to the problems of exploiting raw materials from the environment, is referred to as a technology.
Feminism	Feminism is a diverse collection of social theories, political movements and moral philosophies, largely motivated by or concerned with the experiences of women.
Authority	Authority refers to power that is attached to a position that others perceive as legitimate.

Census	A census is the process of obtaining information about every member of a population. It can be contrasted with sampling in which information is only obtained from a subset of a population. As such it is a method used for accumulating statistical data, and it is also vital to democracy.
Society	A society is a grouping of individuals, which is characterized by common interest and may have distinctive culture and institutions.
Social change	Social change refers to alteration in social structures or culture over time.
Attitude	Attitude refers to an enduring mental representation of a person, place, or thing that evokes an emotional response and related behavior.
Social structure	The term social structure, used in a general sense, refers to entities or groups in definite relation to each other, to relatively enduring patterns of behavior and relationship within social systems, or to social institutions and norms becoming embedded into social systems in such a way that they shape the behavior of actors within those social systems.
Gender	Gender refers to socially defined behavior regarded as appropriate for the members of each
Religiosity	Religiosity refers to a sociological concept referring to the importance of religion in individuals lives.
Social group	A group that consists of two or more people who interact frequently and share a common identity and a feeling of interdependence, is referred to as a social group.
Division of labor	Division of labor is the specialisation of cooperative labor in specific, circumscribed tasks and roles, intended to increase efficiency of output.
Community	Community refers to a group of people who share a common sense of identity and interact with one another on a sustained basis.
Cult	In religion and sociology, a cult is a cohesive group of people (sometimes a relatively small and recently founded religious movement, sometimes numbering in the hundreds of thousands) devoted to beliefs or practices that the surrounding culture or society considers to be far outside the mainstream, sometimes reaching the point of a taboo.
Dyad	A dyad is a group of two people. It usually refers to parents and friends, occasionally to twins.
Authority	Authority refers to power that is attached to a position that others perceive as legitimate.
Denomination	The third most powerful type of religious institution, with a membership generally dominated by a single social class, a formal but not bureaucratic role structure, a trained clergy, traditional authority, abstract relatively unemotional ritual, and a condition of coexistence between it and dominant political and economic institutions, is referred to as a denomination.
Feminism	Feminism is a diverse collection of social theories, political movements and moral philosophies, largely motivated by or concerned with the experiences of women.
Diaspora	The dispersal of an ethnic population from an original homeland into foreign areas, often in a forced manner or under traumatic circumstances, is referred to as a diaspora.
Mode	In statistics, mode means the most frequent value assumed by a random variable, or occurring in a sampling of a random variable.
Reform movement	A reform movement is a kind of social movement that aims to make gradual change, or change in certain aspects of the society rather than rapid or fundamental changes.
Organization	In sociology organization is understood as planned, coordinated and purposeful action of human beings to construct or compile a common tangible or intangible product or service.

Ritual	A ritual is a set of actions, performed mainly for their symbolic value, which is prescribed by a religion or by the traditions of a community.
Sexism	Sexism is commonly considered to be discrimination and/or hatred against people based on their sex rather than their individual merits, but can also refer to any and all systemic differentiations based on the sex of the individuals.
Norm	In sociology, a norm, or social norm, is a rule that is socially enforced. Social sanctioning is what distinguishes norms from other cultural products such as meaning and values.
Discrimination	Discrimination refers to the denial of equal access to social resources to people on the basis of their group membership.
Abortion	An abortion is the removal or expulsion of an embryo or fetus from the uterus, resulting in, or caused by, its death. This can occur spontaneously as a miscarriage, or be artificially induced through chemical, surgical or other means. Commonly, " abortion " refers to an induced procedure at any point in the pregnancy; medically, it is defined as a miscarriage or induced termination before twenty weeks gestation, which is considered nonviable.
Artificial Insemination	Injection of sperm cells into the woman's vagina or uterus for the purpose of inducing pregnancy is defined as artificial insemination.
Consciousness	The awareness of the senzations, thoughts, and feelings being experienced at a given moment is referred to as consciousness.
Median	The number that falls halfway in a range of numbers, or the score below which are half the scores and above which are the other half is a median.
Glass ceiling	Glass ceiling refers to barriers based on attitudinal or organizational bias that prevent qualified females from advancing to top-level positions.
Innovations	A concept created by Robert Merton to describe the way norms assist in achieving goals are referred to as innovations.
Coalition	A coalition is an alliance among entities, during which they cooperate in joint action, each in their own self-interest. This alliance may be temporary or a matter of convenience.
Middle class	A social class broadly defined occupationally as those working in white-collar and lower managerial occupations and is sometimes defined by reference to income levels or subjective identification of the participants in the study are referred to as middle class.
Polyandry	A form of marriage in which a woman may have more than one husband is a polyandry.
Patriarchy	Patriarchy is the anthropological term used to define the sociological condition where male members of a society tend to predominate in positions of power; with the more powerful the position, the more likely it is that a male will hold that position.
Public sphere	Public sphere refers to the means by which people communicate in modern societies, the most prominent component of which is mass media-movies, television, radio, videos, records, magazines, and newspapers.
Range	A measure of variability defined as the high score in a distribution minus the low score is referred to as a range.
Sect	A religious group that draws most members by persuasion from the lower class, that has an informal structure and an untrained clergy, is governed with minimal authority, has few formal rituals, involves spontaneous displays of emotion, and generally opposes the dominant institutions of its society is a sect.
Modernization	The process of general social change brought about by the transition from an agrarian to an industrial mode of production, is referred to as modernization.

Rebellion	A rebellion is, in the most general sense, a refusal to accept authority. It may therefore be seen as encompassing a range of behaviors from civil disobedience to a violent organized attempt to destroy established authority. It is often used in reference to armed resistance against an established government, but can also refer to mass nonviolent resistance movements.
Imperialism	Imperialism is a policy of extending control or authority over foreign entities as a means of acquisition and/or maintenance of empires. This is either through direct territorial conquest or settlement, or through indirect methods of exerting control on the politics and/or economy of these other entities.
Fundamentalism	Fundamentalism has come to refer to several different understandings of religious thought and practice, through literal interpretation of religious texts such as the Bible or the Qur'an and sometimes also anti-modernist movements in various religions.
Liberation theology	An activist Catholic religious movement that combines Catholic beliefs with a passion for social justice for the poor is referred to as liberation theology.
Government	A government is a body that has the authority to make and the power to enforce laws within a civil, corporate, religious, academic, or other organization or group.
Separate spheres	The belief that women are naturally suited to tend private homes and nurture children, whereas men are naturally suited to participate in public affairs and earn mone is referred to as separate spheres.
Ideology	Ideology refers to shared ideas or beliefs which serve to justify and support the interests of a particular group or organizations.
Technology	The application of logic, reason and knowledge to the problems of exploiting raw materials from the environment, is referred to as a technology.
Status quo	Status quo is a Latin term meaning the present, current, existing state of affairs. To maintain the status quo is to keep things the way they presently are.
Neighborhood	A neighborhood is a geographically localized community located within a larger city, town or suburb. Traditionally, a neighborhood is small enough that the neighbors are all able to know each other.
Religious movement	An association of people who join together to seek to spread a new religion or to promote a new interpretation of an existing religion is a religious movement.
Reconstruction	Reconstruction refers to a memory that is not an exact replica of an event but has been pieced together from a few highlights, using information that may or may not be accurate.
Dualism	Dualism refers to the philosophical theory that two distinct systems, the material body and the immaterial soul-are involved in the control of behavior.
Racism	Racism is a belief in the moral or biological superiority of one race or ethnic group over another or others.
Bias	A bias is a prejudice in a general or specific sense, usually in the sense for having a preference to one particular point of view or ideological perspective.
Social class	A category of people who occupy a similar position in relation to the means through which goods and services are produced in a society is a social class.
Sexual orientation	Sexual orientation describes the direction of an individual's sexuality, often in relation to their own sex or gender. Common terms for describing sexual orientation include bisexual (bi), heterosexual (straight) and homosexual (lesbian/gay).

Go to **Cram101.com** for the Practice Tests for this Chapter.

Census	A census is the process of obtaining information about every member of a population. It can be contrasted with sampling in which information is only obtained from a subset of a population. As such it is a method used for accumulating statistical data, and it is also vital to democracy.
Demographics	The analysis of data used by advertizing agencies to target an audience by sex, age, income level, marital status, geographic location, and occupation are referred to as demographics.
Social class	A category of people who occupy a similar position in relation to the means through which goods and services are produced in a society is a social class.
Gender	Gender refers to socially defined behavior regarded as appropriate for the members of each
Industrialized societies	Strongly developed nation-states in which the majority of the population work in factories or offices rather than in agriculture, and most people live in urban areas are referred to as industrialized societies.
Society	A society is a grouping of individuals, which is characterized by common interest and may have distinctive culture and institutions.
Life expectancy	The number of years a newborn in a particular society can expect to live is referred to as a life expectancy.
Variable	A characteristic that varies in value or magnitude along which an object, individual or group may be categorized, such as income or age, is referred to as a variable.
Obesity	The state of being more than 20 percent above the average weight for a person of one's height is referred to as an obesity.
Social support	Social support is the physical and emotional comfort given to us by our family, friends, co-workers and others. It is knowing that we are part of a community of people who love and care for us, and value and think well of us.
Marital status	A person's marital status describes their relationship with a significant other. Some common statuses are: married, single, separated, divorced, widowed, engaged, invalid, annulled, living common-law. The number of children may also be specified and, in this case, becomes synonymous with family status. For example: married with no children. Marital status is often a question on censuses, credit card applications, and many different polls.
Conformity	Conformity is the act of consciously maintaining a certain degree of similarity (in clothing, manners, behaviors, etc.) to those in your general social circles, to those in authority, or to the general status quo. Usually, conformity implies a tendency to submit to others in thought and behavior other than simply clothing choice.
Stereotype	A stereotype refers to widely shared beliefs about the characteristic traits, attitudes, and behaviors of members of various social groups, including the assumption that the members of such groups are usually all alike.
Mortality rate	Mortality rate is a measure of the number of deaths in some population, scaled to the size of that population, per unit time. Mortality rate is typically expressed in units of deaths per 1000 individuals per year; thus, a mortality rate of 10000.5 in a population of 100,000 would mean 1,000,500 deaths per year in the entire population.
Statistics	Statistics is a mathematical science pertaining to the collection, analysis, interpretation, and presentation of data. It is applicable to a wide variety of academic disciplines, from the physical and social sciences to the humanities; it is also used and misused for making informed decisions in all areas of business and government.
Masculinity	Masculinity refers to the characteristic forms of behavior expected of men in any given culture.

Gender role	A gender role is a set of behavioral norms associated with males and with females, respectively, in a given social group or system.
Sector	Sector refers to parts of the economy as judged by the economic activity that they constitute. For example agriculture, forestry, fishing and mining constitute the primary sector.
Median	The number that falls halfway in a range of numbers, or the score below which are half the scores and above which are the other half is a median.
Discrimination	Discrimination refers to the denial of equal access to social resources to people on the basis of their group membership.
Racism	Racism is a belief in the moral or biological superiority of one race or ethnic group over another or others.
Murder	Murder is the unlawful, premeditated killing of a human being by another. The penalty for murder is usually either life imprisonment, or in jurisdictions with capital punishment, the death penalty.
Robbery	The unlawful taking of, or the attempt to take something of value from another person or persons by using violence or the threat of violence, is referred to as a robbery.
Domestic violence	Domestic violence occurs when a family member, partner or ex-partner attempts to physically or psychologically dominate or harm the other.
Sexism	Sexism is commonly considered to be discrimination and/or hatred against people based on their sex rather than their individual merits, but can also refer to any and all systemic differentiations based on the sex of the individuals.
Crime	Crime refers to any action that violates criminal laws established by political authority. A crime in a nontechnical sense is an act that violates a very important political or moral command.
Sexual orientation	Sexual orientation describes the direction of an individual's sexuality, often in relation to their own sex or gender. Common terms for describing sexual orientation include bisexual (bi), heterosexual (straight) and homosexual (lesbian/gay).
Bisexual	Bisexual is the sexual orientation which refers to the aesthetic, romantic, or sexual desire for individuals of either gender or of either sex.
Community	Community refers to a group of people who share a common sense of identity and interact with one another on a sustained basis.
Cocaine	Cocaine is a crystalline tropane alkaloid that is obtained from the leaves of the coca plant. It is a stimulant of the central nervous system and an appetite suppressant, creating what has been described as a euphoric sense of happiness and increased energy.
Sexually transmitted disease	Disease transmitted through sexual contact is a sexually transmitted disease.
Stigmatized	People who have been negatively labeled because of their participation, or alleged participation, in deviant or outlawed behaviors are referred to as stigmatized.
Prejudice	Prejudice is, as the name implies, the process of "pre-judging" something. It implies coming to a judgment on a subject before learning where the preponderance of evidence actually lies, or forming a judgment without direct experience.
Social network	A social network is a social structure made of nodes which are generally individuals or organizations. It indicates the ways in which they are connected through various social

familiarities ranging from casual acquaintance to close familial bonds.

Social isolation	A type of loneliness that occurs when a person lacks a sense of integrated involvement. Being deprived of participation in a group or community involving companionship, shared interests, organized activities, and meaningful roles causes a person to feel is a social isolation.
Disability	A physical or health condition that stigmatizes or causes discrimination, is referred to as a disability.
Poverty line	The poverty threshold, or poverty line, is the level of income below which one cannot afford to purchase all the resources one requires to live. Thus, by definition, nobody lives below the poverty line.
Norm	In sociology, a norm, or social norm, is a rule that is socially enforced. Social sanctioning is what distinguishes norms from other cultural products such as meaning and values.
Femininity	Femininity comprises the physical and mental attributes associated with the female sex and is partly culturally determined.
Sick role	Sick role was a concept invented by Talcott Parsons that refers to patterns of behavior expected of one who is sick and this role often exempts the person from their normal role obligations.
Curative medicine	Curative medicine is another term for Crisis Medicine, in which the focus is on curing disease rather than its prevention.
Public sphere	Public sphere refers to the means by which people communicate in modern societies, the most prominent component of which is mass media-movies, television, radio, videos, records, magazines, and newspapers.
Technology	The application of logic, reason and knowledge to the problems of exploiting raw materials from the environment, is referred to as a technology.
Government	A government is a body that has the authority to make and the power to enforce laws within a civil, corporate, religious, academic, or other organization or group.
Medicalization	The process through which medical perspectives and treatment become increasingly influential and common in a society, is referred to as medicalization.
Depression	In the field of psychiatry, the word depression can also have this meaning of low mood but more specifically refers to a mental illness when it has reached a severity and duration to warrant a diagnosis, whether there is an obvious situational cause or not.
Abortion	An abortion is the removal or expulsion of an embryo or fetus from the uterus, resulting in, or caused by, its death. This can occur spontaneously as a miscarriage, or be artificially induced through chemical, surgical or other means. Commonly, " abortion " refers to an induced procedure at any point in the pregnancy; medically, it is defined as a miscarriage or induced termination before twenty weeks gestation, which is considered nonviable.
Attitude	Attitude refers to an enduring mental representation of a person, place, or thing that evokes an emotional response and related behavior.
Ageism	Ageism refers to prejudice against a person on the grounds of age in the belief that the age category is inferior to other age categories and that unequal treatment is therefore justified.
Sexual harassment	Sexual harassment refers to the making of persistent unwanted sexual advances by one individual towards another.
Patriarchal family	Patriarchal family refers to a family in which the father is head of the household with authority over other family members.

Prestige	Prestige refers to social respect accorded to an individual or group because of the status of their position.
Affirmative action	Government programs intended to assure minorities and women equal hiring or admission opportunities is referred to as affirmative action.
Intake	Intake refers to process during which a juvenile referral is received and a decision is made to file a petition in juvenile court to release the juvenile, to place the juvenile under supervision, or to refer the juvenile elsewhere.
Organization	In sociology organization is understood as planned, coordinated and purposeful action of human beings to construct or compile a common tangible or intangible product or service.
Labeling	Labeling is defining or describing a person in terms of his or her behavior. The term is often used in sociology to describe human interaction, control and identification of deviant behavior.
Content analysis	Content analysis refers to analysis of words and images contained in written, spoken, and visual media.
Stereotyping	Stereotyping refers to a process whereby a trait, usually negative, is generalized to all members of a particular group.
Psychoactive drug	A drug that alters normal mental functioning-mood, perception, or thought; called a controlled substance if used medically is a psychoactive drug.
Dysfunction	Dysfunction refers to an institution's negative impact on the sociocultural system.
Personality disorder	Personality disorder refers to a mental disorder characterized by a set of inflexible, maladaptive personality traits that keep a person from functioning properly in society.
Aversion Therapy	A behavior therapy in which an aversive stimulus is paired with an undesirable behavior until the behavior becomes associated with pain and discomfort is an aversion therapy.
Social mobility	Social mobility is the degree to which, in a given society, an individual's social status can change throughout the course of his or her life, or the degree to which that individual's offspring and subsequent generations move up and down the class system.
Bias	A bias is a prejudice in a general or specific sense, usually in the sense for having a preference to one particular point of view or ideological perspective.
Learned helplessness	A model for the acquisition of depressive behavior, based on findings that organisms in aversive situations learn to show inactivity when their operants go unreinforced is learned helplessness.
Socialization	Socialization refers to the lifelong processes through which humans develop an awareness of social norms and values, and achieve a distinct sense of self.
Social status	Social status refers to a position in a social relationship, a characteristic that locates individuals in relation to other people and sets of role expectations.
Agoraphobia	Agoraphobia is the fear of having a panic attack in general in any place whether it be the grocer, at work or in the privacy of your own home.
Rebellion	A rebellion is, in the most general sense, a refusal to accept authority. It may therefore be seen as encompassing a range of behaviors from civil disobedience to a violent organized attempt to destroy established authority. It is often used in reference to armed resistance against an established government, but can also refer to mass nonviolent resistance movements.
Taboo	A taboo is a strong social prohibition (or ban) relating to any area of human activity or social custom declared as sacred and forbidden; breaking of the taboo is usually considered

objectionable or abhorrent by society.

Dominance	In animal colonies, a condition established by one animal over another by prevailing in an aggressive encounter between the two, is referred to as dominance.
Alcoholism	Alcoholism refers to a disorder that involves long-term, repeated, uncontrolled, compulsive, and excessive use of alcoholic beverages and that impairs the drinker's health, work and social relationships.
Homophobia	Homophobia is the fear of, aversion to, or discrimination against homosexuality or homosexuals. It can also mean hatred, hostility, or disapproval of homosexual people, sexual behavior, or cultures, and is generally used to assert bigotry.
Alienation	In sociology and critical social theory, alienation refers to the individual's estrangement from traditional community and others in general.
Educational attainment	Educational attainment is a term commonly used by statisticans to refer to the highest degree of education an individual has completed.
Sexual double standard	The belief that men have exclusive rights of erotic access to women without women possessing reciprocal exclusive rights of erotic access to men is a sexual double standard.
Double standard	A double standard is a standard applied more leniently to one group than to another. A double standard violates this principle by holding different people accountable according to different standards.
Coping	Efforts to control, reduce, or learn to tolerate the threats that lead to stress is referred to as coping.
Punishment	Punishment is the practice of imposing something unpleasant on a subject as a response to some unwanted behavior or disobedience that the subject has displayed.
Child abuse	Child abuse refers to not only physical assaults on a child but also malnourishment, abandonment, neglect, emotional abuse and sexual abuse.
Extended family	Extended family refers to a family group consisting of more than two generations of the same kinship line living either within the same household or, more usually in the west, very close to one another.
Addiction	A pattern of behavior characterized by an overwhelming involvement with using a drug and securing its supply is defined as an addiction.
Antidepressant	An antidepressant is a medication designed to treat or alleviate the symptoms of clinical depression. Some, notably the tricyclics, are commonly used off-label in the treatment of neuropathic pain, whether or not the patient is depressed. Smaller doses are generally used for this purpose, and they often take effect more quickly.
Socioeconomic status	An overall rank based on characteristics such as education and occupation, used to describe people's positions in stratification systems is referred to as socioeconomic status.
Status quo	Status quo is a Latin term meaning the present, current, existing state of affairs. To maintain the status quo is to keep things the way they presently are.
Drug therapy	Control of psychological problems through drugs is referred to as drug therapy.
Incest	Incest is sexual activity between close family members. Incest is considered taboo, and forbidden (fully or slightly) in the majority of current cultures.
Human rights	Human rights refers to natural and inalienable rights accorded to all human beings, such as the right to life, liberty, and happiness. They also may include rights essential to a dignified human existence, such as freedom of movement, free speech, a good education, employment.

Go to **Cram101.com** for the Practice Tests for this Chapter.

Authority	Authority refers to power that is attached to a position that others perceive as legitimate.
Social change	Social change refers to alteration in social structures or culture over time.
Social structure	The term social structure, used in a general sense, refers to entities or groups in definite relation to each other, to relatively enduring patterns of behavior and relationship within social systems, or to social institutions and norms becoming embedded into social systems in such a way that they shape the behavior of actors within those social systems.

Go to **Cram101.com** for the Practice Tests for this Chapter.

91

Go to **Cram101.com** for the Practice Tests for this Chapter.
And, **NEVER** highlight a book again!

UNIVERSITY OF WOLVERHAMPTON

Printed in the United States
97249LV00002B/307/A